Divination 101

How to intuitively read oracle and tarot cards

The only book you'll need to develop your psychic
abilities while learning to read the cards

Anne-Marie   6th Sense Connection

© Copyright 2022 – 6th Sense Connection. All rights reserved.
ISBN: 978-0-9998971-1-9

This book is copyright protected and is only for personal use. You cannot amend, distribute, sell, use, quote or paraphrase any part of the content within this book without the consent and permission of the author or publisher. The author assumes no responsibility for your actions or choices before, during or after reading this workbook or using the 6th Sense Connection Oracle Cards or any other card decks. Under no circumstance will the author or the publisher accept legal responsibility or blame for any reparation, damages or monetary loss due to the information herein, either directly or indirectly. The author intends to provide you with general information and education and hopes this workbook, used with Oracle or Tarot Cards, will assist you on your spiritual journey of self-discovery.

Published and distributed in the USA by 6th Sense Connection LLC
Author: Anne-Marie   6th Sense Connection

DISCLAIMER:
Readings are for entertainment purposes only. This information is not presented by a medical practitioner or an attorney and is only for informational purposes. The content is not intended to be a substitute for professional legal advice, medical advice, diagnosis or treatment. Always seek the advice of your legal representative or your healthcare provider with any questions you may have regarding any legal issues or medical conditions. Never disregard legal, professional or medical advice or delay seeking it because of something you have read.

Dedication

A special dedication and thank you to the following loved ones...

Nicholas McCormack
Christopher McCormack
Brian Edwards
Mum and Dad
Tracy Piddington
Nicole Salvador
Kimilia Klosinski
Kim Muller
Sherre Wellins
Trish Smith
Teketa Shine
Tricia Jones
Kayla Winter
Andrew Hamer

And especially, The Infinite Spirit, my lost loved ones and the Angels.

Contents

7   **Introduction**

        Secrets to successful intuitive card readings

9   **Part 1 - Getting started**

    10   Wishful thinking or intuition
    13   Nothing to fear except fear itself
    14   Exercise - excuses
    15   Exercise - create new habits
    17   Your intuitive superpower
    21   Exercise - trust your intuition
    22   Protector and saboteur
    23   Receiving intuitive messages
    25   Natural psychic abilities
    26   Psychic from birth

28   **Part 2 - Out of your mind**

    30   Your spiritual toolbox
    31   Exercise - visualize
    34   More ways to connect
    34   Singing and dancing
    35   Candles and journaling
    36   Grounding meditation
    37   Connecting your intuition with your cards

40   Part 3 - Readings

- 41   Shuffling the cards
- 42   When reading for others
- 43   Reading disclosures
- 44   Preparing to do readings
- 46   How to prepare
- 47   During a reading
- 51   Akashic record readings
- 53   Reverse card meanings
- 54   When the connection becomes cloudy
- 55   If you are not connecting
- 55   When your reading is complete
- 56   Strengthening your intuitive connection
- 60   Caring for your cards
- 62   Retiring your cards
- 63   Obtaining cards

65   Part 4 - Questions and card spreads

- 65   Phrasing questions
- 65   One question leads to another
- 66   Examples and questions
- 67   When to use card spreads
- 67   Three card spread
- 69   Five card spread
- 71   Six cards with a wild card spread
- 73   The year ahead spread
- 74   The Celtic Cross

77   Part 5 - "Life happens while we make other plans" - John Lennon

- 84   Bad things happen to good people
- 86   Exercise - three card story
- 88   What is your life purpose?
- 90   Different life purposes

94   About the author

Introduction

Secrets to successful intuitive card readings

Are you ready to work on your intuition while learning to read cards intuitively? This exciting journey is all about making some important discoveries while learning at your own pace. The easy-to-follow instructions and exercises will show you how to awaken the divine connection that has always been within you. You are part of the universe and encouraged to explore this incredible connection and what it can do to enrich your life.

This workbook has four goals...
1. Help you read tarot or oracle cards intuitively and take your readings to the next level
2. Getting out of your head and staying in the zone while activating your intuition
3. Composing your questions to receive answers that are crystal clear
4. Break through some of your blockages and discover your hidden potential

I have been reading cards professionally since the early 1980s. In this workbook I'll share my secrets of maintaining your intuitive connection while reading cards. You may be trying to tap into your intuition when you read cards but need a little help getting out of your head and staying in the zone.

I'll show you a few easy learning and practice techniques. These will help you get out of your head and strengthen your intuitive energy naturally. During this process, you will be able to unravel some of life's little mysteries and find answers to the questions that may have eluded you. Ensure you keep good notes to see how far you have come on this magical journey. The 6th Sense Connection Oracle

Cards are a great tool to use while exploring and expanding your intuitive connection with the divine however, you could use your favorite tarot or oracle card deck. All types of tarot and oracle cards can be used as a bridge to help you build and strengthen this magical connection.

Be prepared for some significant shifts and changes, as the insights you will receive can be life-changing. When you become skilled at connecting with your intuitive side, you'll find valuable insights that should help you take your readings to a higher level. If you are a professional card reader, this book has a lot of content that you will find helpful. Join us on this exciting journey of self-discovery. There is no time like the present to change things to your advantage!

I'll be using the 6th Sense Connection Oracle Cards for all the exercises in this book.

If you do not have a deck, you can get them from our website

www.6thsenseconnection.com/onlineshop

or Amazon through this link   **https://bit.ly/6thsenseoraclecards**

or all good bookstores.

Part 1

Getting started

The card decks you feel drawn to are the ones you should work with when learning how to take your readings to the next level. The right deck will seem to speak to you and you feel drawn to unlock their wisdom. You may have other decks and for unknown reasons, you do not feel tempted to use them. Put them aside for now as it is not the right time to work with them.

The card decks you want to work with are the right tools to develop your special connection. Think of these cards as your new best friend. Their images have started to speak to you and the more you work with them, the more you will be able to connect with mystical wisdom.

Use this deck to help you build your special relationship with your intuition. Keep the guidebook that came with your cards handy and read it through a couple of times. There could be pearls of wisdom hidden within its pages. The author may be able to share some unique insights about their card deck that will help you form a bond with these cards.

As this journey progresses, you'll start to depend on your intuition more and refer to the guidebook less. Once you are comfortable calling upon your intuition, you'll develop your meanings for the cards. You may find they are akin to memories, people you have met and situations you have experienced.

Bear in mind that these meanings are not cast in stone either. Depending on other factors, they will change with what the Angels or Spirit Guides tell you and what you're sensing during the session.

You might already be using your intuition but often second-guessing what you perceive. It happens when you have activated your human mind and slipped back into the logical side of your brain.

Wishful thinking or intuition

Maybe you wonder if what you are sensing could be wishful thinking or could it be your fears or anxieties surfacing instead of your hopes and dreams? You'll find it helpful to learn how to get out of your usual way of reading and get your brain to accept and acknowledge your intuitive side.

Could it be your imagination running away with you or is it your intuition and how do you tell the difference?

The first step is to accept that our imagination is also an essential part of us. Allowing it to work with us instead of against us will help us become 'Inspired,' which is a massive step in activating our intuition. Imagination and intuition both dwell in the creative side of our brain and our imagination sparks our creative energy, which is an integral part of our divine essence.

Once activated, this helps us open up to see and sense things with the mind's eye, often referred to as our third eye. You'll find yours between your eyebrows in the center of your forehead; we'll work on opening it up and using it to your advantage. It helps to imagine seeing your third eye opening during mini-meditations. Soon, you will start to see different perspectives in your every day world.

This amazing information is yours by divine right. The key unlocks the door to becoming 'Inspired.' People often ask me how to tell the difference between intuition and imagination?

Our imagination can be fanciful or put the fear of God into us. Our intuition on the other hand, brings clear, intuitive messages.

Here are some ways to tell the difference

1. Your intuition never speaks badly about you
2. Its purpose is to keep you safe while pointing you in the right direction
3. Your intuition will not imply that you are not good enough or strong enough
4. It will lovingly encourage you to be all that you can be

Imagination
To get into the zone say, "I am creative and inspiration flows through me with love, grace and ease"

Exercise - know the difference between your imagination, wishful thinking and inspiration.

Recall a time when you thought you were experiencing wishful thinking when in reality it was your intuition. What would you have done differently and how would you change this in the future?

....
....
....
....
....
....
....
....
....
....
....
....
....
....
....
....
....
....
....
....
....
....
....
....
....
....
....

Remember: Your intuition will never talk badly about you!

Nothing to fear except fear itself

Although it may not seem like it, more often than not, there is nothing to fear except fear itself. When your mind starts spiralling into fearful thoughts and feelings, tell it to stop! Next, choose to change your focus to loving thoughts and feelings. You can do this by reliving a memory of when you felt happy.

This happy memory trumps anything negative. Tell your mind you are becoming inspired now. You understand that doing something new can be scary. You might hear it say, "What if we fail?" Turn that around by saying, "What if we succeed?" There is no time like the present to get started!

A few examples of the lies your imagination might tell you.

It is a load of rubbish; how can cards tell you anything?
People will think you have gone mad
You are not psychic, so stop wasting your time
It may be a good idea but not for you, maybe you should think about doing something else
Tomorrow might be a better day to make a change
What if you see something that scares you?
You are not important enough for others to listen to what you have to say

It is time to get your imagination to work with you instead of against you. Write three of the top excuses your imagination gives you that cause you to stop making progress.
These are some of my imagination lies, how about yours?

I do not have the time to learn new things
My life is fine the way it is, so why rock the boat?
Facing my fears will not be easy, better to do it tomorrow

Does any of this sound familiar?

Exercise - Excuses

Write down the best excuses you use to stop yourself from making positive changes. Be as open and honest with yourself as possible. For every excuse you have, there is a simple method to turn it around into something positive. I often tell myself, I have heard enough bullshit today. I rephrase those negative excuses into positive solutions. In other words, you can turn those excuses into helpful positive affirmations.

For example, thinking "I do not have time to do this now", can be replaced by "I will use my time more wisely. It's part of my path that I grow and learn. I plan to do less of X, so I have time to do Y, which will make me feel better about myself."

List some of your examples

....
....
....
....
....
....
....
....
....
....
....
....
....
....
....
....
....
....
....
....

Exercise - Create new habits

A great way to start a new habit is by replacing an old habit with a new one, for instance, instead of watching the news or having the TV on in the background, set up your smart TV, laptop or phone to watch or listen to motivational talks or upbeat, happy music while doing other tasks. It is about learning to do things differently and making them part of your routine. When you adopt a new healthy habit, piggyback it onto an older practice already part of your routine. You're more likely to stick to it by making this simple change.

Try it for a day and if it works, do it for a week; you'll see the positive changes you've already manifested and it was effortless. Ensure you keep notes in your journal to share what worked for you.

Well done! You have turned down the nagging voice of doubt. When your mind comes up with another excuse, refer back to these pages to turn 'Why you cannot do something' into 'Why you can!'

Over the page, write down all the new excuses that your mind finds and switch them from negative reasons into positive affirmations, this will help you succeed.

Write down some habits you are willing to change to become something more productive.

Your intuitive superpower

Our intuition is exclusively ours alone. We see and sense things differently than everyone else. Just like our fingerprints, our intuition is unique. Our Angels, Spirit Guides and lost loved ones send us intuitive messages in a way that they feel we will be able to understand them. There are some things that we will all share when using our intuition. Does any of the following sound familiar?

1. Sometimes, you just know when something is going to happen. When this occurs, you have tapped into your sixth sense naturally. You know it is your sixth sense as it is a 'deep knowing' that your logical mind cannot explain. The goal is to strengthen this natural form of communication.
2. What about when we meet a person for the first time and instantly dislike them? We hear the voice of doubt, sending signals that we cannot trust this person. No matter how much you argue with yourself, there is an inner knowing that we should not trust this person. We tell ourselves it is just our imagination. We know it's not logical to judge a book by its cover but that nagging voice of doubt continues. How could we feel such a feeling of apprehension from someone we have never met before? We tell ourselves we are being silly and have allowed our imagination to run away with us. That gut feeling came straight from the divine and it needs to be trusted. We get these feelings for an excellent reason, which is not apparent at that moment but will become clear in time.
3. What about when you are walking or driving and suddenly feel an urge to change your route? Change the way to your destination and you will either see someone you have not seen in ages or avoid someone or something for the same reason!

Sometimes, these divine messages can be for a serious reason. Later, we find out that we may have been in an accident had we traveled on our original route.

1. All intuitive messages are sent from the divine and enter your being through your sixth sense. It is your spiritual GPS and you will feel it in your gut, hear voices or see with your mind's eye and gain insight that has no apparent explanation, yet it would be wise to trust it.
2. When your phone rings and you know who is calling before you answer, perhaps you get a strong urge to call someone and find out they need some help or advice. There are many more examples I could give you, but I'm sure you get the idea.

Without trying, your brain has access to the five senses of sight, hearing, smell, taste and touch. It has forgotten how to naturally access your sixth sense and the signals and messages it sends. Your sixth sense does not originate from your brain and your brain thinks it is the only part of your body capable of processing intelligent information. Naturally, it goes into denial because we believe it is just our imagination. You are an adult of sound mind and thought. You are not crazy! You are competent in the use of logic, reasoning and intelligence. So why should you trust any information that did not originate in the brain?

Is it logical to put yourself on guard when you have received a weird feeling or voice in your head advising you should not be going down the road you are currently traveling? Then comes the internal dilemma and you find yourself arguing with yourself over the information you received. You try to shake it off and dismiss it. You might think you are being paranoid or blowing things up out of proportion but by ignoring these critical messages, you dull your sixth sense.

If we go back to the phone analogy, we did not answer the call, instead we let it go to voice mail and later deleted the message as an unsolicited call containing misleading information. Why not start trusting these messages or have an open mind towards them? Tell your brain this message came from the divine and that you should listen to it. Its purpose is to help you somehow and all will become clear in time. Trust the messenger and the message and keep an open mind about how the information will unfold.

Remember that person you met and your intuition told you not to trust them? Well, perhaps you told them something in confidence they told everyone. It's a good job it was nothing important that needed to be kept secret. In time, people will show you who they really are, will they have to betray your trust in some way before you trust your intuition? Even if we give them the benefit of the doubt they may think they can keep your secrets but the people they tell them to cannot. The intuitive message was right and this person must not be confided in or be trusted.

Your sixth sense connects you to the divine and every living thing on the earth. Consider that all living things on the planet are connected. Once you learn to tap into your intuitive nature and listen to it regularly, it will grow stronger. The help it can provide you is invaluable and you will soon wonder why everyone is not doing this. Encouraging your intuition to develop will be a tremendous advantage in so many ways in your life. Like everything else we start to learn, it takes time, practice and patience. The rewards it brings will outweigh the investment in time it takes to nurture the intuition. Our thoughts and feelings can get in the way of our connection to our sixth sense.

When we start analyzing and rationalizing what we are sensing we cloud our connection to the source. Avoid trying to clarify or translate these messages, they will make sense in time. There is no logic to be applied as this will get in the way and you may lose the very essence of the message. It's best to accept messages as they are delivered, translating or rationalizing them could also dilute the meaning and you could end up missing the real message completely.

During the very act of rationalization, your brain gets involved and you lose your crystal-clear connection. Think of it as if someone called you on the phone and the line was excellent at the start of the conversation. Then you added another party to the call and the phone line became all fuzzy with static so you are no longer sure what you are picking up at all. The connection becomes strained and the line becomes weak and breaks up. It would be wise to hang up and try your call later. When you decide against your intuition and do the opposite of what it told you, most situations will worsen before they get better.

Psychic Empath
You need to be listening
to your intuition

Exercise - Trust your intuition

Take a few minutes to write and remind yourself when you should have trusted your intuition and things did not work out as planned.

Protector and saboteur

Our ego has many facets and is not just an over-inflated view of ourselves and our 'need to be right'. It is another critical part of us and one of the ways we use it is to protect ourselves against those who would harm us. We know it as the nagging voice of doubt that we hear when we begin to work with our intuition. It tells you the logical choice is the right one to make because what went wrong in the past could go wrong in the future. It is no wonder that we mistakenly trust our ego and, by doing so, we screw up! Do not let these fears stop you from living your best life. Consider your past and decide to do things differently as you have learned from your mistakes.

Remember, all is not lost, you can consult your intuition via your cards. You can find your way out of the maze you created by trusting 'the intuitive inner voice.' Do not allow your ego to become dominant when intuition tells you something different.

Next, forgive yourself for making a mistake. When we make it hard to forgive ourselves, we are wrapped up in our ego and continue to punish ourselves for being human and making mistakes. We need to lovingly decide to chalk this up to experience and let it go.

Consider you were worried about doing what was good for you and were wrapped up in the story of what could be and became deaf to your intuitive messages. The choice you made was clearly on your path for a reason. It was a lesson to be learned and sometimes we have to learn things the hard way.

Receiving intuitive messages

You can receive intuitive messages in a variety of ways. It is not always a strong feeling in your gut however, this is a primary way to receive important notifications from the divine. There are other ways you can connect with the Source, the Universe, Angels or intuitive energy, lost loved ones, your Higher Self, Ascended Masters and more. Look at what you see every day and slow down. Pay attention to the people you are interacting with; are they in distress or do they seem at ease? There are many ways we receive intuitive information about what is happening around us.

Look up at the sky, do you see faces in the clouds? Does it seem like there is an animated painting unfolding before your eyes? If so, what is it telling you?

What about your current situation? Is there a song on the radio or a story on the news that seems to resonate with what's going on a with you? Is the subject coming up in another way during your day? What messages are you are receiving about your situation and what positive steps can you take to turn things around?

Remember, the analogy of our intuition being like a direct phone line to the divine. Sometimes it is like watching a story unfold on TV screen in our mind's eye. At other times it is like a movie playing with no sound. When we are lucky, we get pictures and sound. There are many Spirit Guides, Angels and Spirits on the other end of the phone. And sometimes we can see them.

You may start noticing and finding signs like feathers, eagles, pennies or butterflies, etc. Allow your heart to jump with joy and thank your Guides, Angels and the Divine for sending the message! You are one of a kind! It is time to figure out the most straightforward way you can naturally connect with your intuition to strengthen your 'telephone line' to the divine.

Once you have mastered one way, you should find it easier to encourage other communication methods with the Divine. It is like body building, your glute exercises may also strengthen your hamstrings. Your spiritual body becomes more robust and receptive to receiving messages.

Everyone on a spiritual journey can benefit from having like-minded friends who share the same goals. It is like having a workout buddy that you meet at the gym, but in this scenario you would chat to each other about your spiritual experiences and share your a-ha moments. Do you have a friend who might be open to getting involved in stretching their psychic muscles? If so, invite them to join you on this exciting journey.

At 6th Sense Connection, we have free Facebook groups where you can meet like-minded people. You can also join our website and sign up for group or private classes. For further information go to www.6thsenseconnection.com. You may find it challenging to share your psychic journey with friends and family that do not feel similarly moved to explore their psychic abilities.

Alternatively, your loved ones may be fascinated by what you are experiencing but have no desire to develop or learn to trust their intuition. However, they will ask you to let them know if you sense anything about them. Either way, your next step is to connect with like-minded people and be open to sharing your experiences with them and vice-versa. It can be a lot of fun finding your tribe, some of them you will feel you have known forever, yet you may have only just met.

Natural psychic abilities

Some of the ways intuitive information is received can be via your natural psychic abilities. Using your psychic perception means you can detect or pick up things by combining one of your senses with another. You may find that one or more of these psychic senses are natural to you and others may develop as you work on your intuition.

Astral Projection – Spiritually travel to other places without leaving the body

Clairvoyant – Their third eye is open and able to see spirits

Clairaudient – Hear things from the unseen world

Clairsentient – Sense the energy of others, AKA a psychic empath

Claircognizance – An immediate deep sense of knowing that something will happen

Clairalience - Being able to smell something that does not have a physical source

Clairgustance - Ability to taste something without putting anything into your mouth

Intuitive – Knowing things about people or places without logical reasoning

Premonition – A strong psychic warning about an event or person that shouldn't be ignored

Psychic manifestation – Ability to think things into reality

Psychic Vampire – Unknowingly drains the energy of others

Psychometry – Senses people, places situations by touching objects

Remote Viewing – Able to see and describe other places accurately without having been there

Telekinesis – The ability to move things with one's mind by directing energy

Psychic from birth

When we are young, we have access to some or all of these abilities. We tend to grow out of using them as we grow up. Sometimes this happens when our parents tell us that the people and things we see are figments of our imagination but as we relax and start to rest our conscious minds, we become more aware of the unseen world. We call out for a parent to come and save us, to get rid of whatever is hiding in the shadows. They say it is just our imagination playing tricks on us because they see nothing when they turn on the light.

So, we start to close down our psychic abilities and shut out the unseen world. Our parents do not see anything, so why should we?

What if we were taught that there is nothing to fear but fear itself. What if we knew that the energy or the spirit we sense is just one of our guardian angels watching over us? What if we imagine that we have flooded the room with beautiful white light when we feel something? How about asking our Guardian Angels to watch over us while we sleep? What happens if we throw an imaginary bucket of light over the presence? Does it make it grow stronger? If so, then the energy we are picking up is from the light.

Any negative energy in the room is driven from the light.

When we perceive these energies in a different light, perhaps we would not be frightened and block them out. We might want to talk to them, find out who they are and thank them for watching over us. When children are disturbed by any spiritual energy at night, it's wise to remove any spiritual gateways or portals in their room. Mirrors, artwork showing another place or time or any likenesses of any religious symbols can be used as portals or gateways. Closing them down should help children to stop seeing things disturbing their sleep.

When you put children to bed, visualize a dome covering their bed that makes them invisible to all and any wandering spirits. Ask Archangel Michael to watch over them while they sleep and use his mighty sword to chase away any unwanted presence by unknown spirits. If, as an adult, your sleep is similarly disturbed, do the same thing. It works just as well for any age group.

Part 2

Out of your mind

You've heard the phrase, 'Two heads are better than one.' Sometimes, we think about asking a friend for their advice about our situation. What would they do if they were in our shoes? This second opinion also comes into play when we argue with ourselves. Do we choose the logical reason or our emotional response?

When people trust logic and ignore their emotions, did they simply choose the logical answer given all the information regarding this subject? They would tell us they have looked at all the data and the only choice to make is the one they believe to be true. Therefore, it is in their best interests to proceed that way. What about the people who make decisions based on their emotional response? Are they letting their heart rule their head or have they weighed up all the pros and cons and decided to take action based on how it makes them feel?

How about when you are in two minds and cannot make a decision? Both thoughts and feelings are part of our human nature. They argue with each other with bias based on our past experiences or what they think might happen. Are we procrastinating because we do not see a good option? What about a third choice, how about listening to your intuition?

Consider that you have two minds. Our human brain represents one and it works in harmony with our five senses, sight, smell, touch, taste and hearing. Our intuitive mind is our sixth sense and dwells in the spiritual energy of our heart. It is a part of our divine essence and our connection to the universal energy source that some call God, Goddess and many other names. I use 'The Infinite Spirit,' which I often shorten to Spirit.

Some people do not believe in intuition at all. Yet, in many professions and situations, intuition is applied and trusted without the user being consciously aware that their intuition is helping them. For example, a doctor wants to run blood tests or body scans without a logical explanation. Despite their years of medical training, they have a gut feeling about a health issue that a patient may be experiencing. It defies logic however, the doctor wants to be able to either confirm or rule out their suspicions.

Our intuitive mind processes mystical and spiritual wisdom. This information comes to us instantly without rational thought or reason. This is not to be confused with a premonition, an uneasy feeling that implies something terrible is about to happen. Premonitions are messages from your spirit guides and angels, meant to keep you safe. It is best to take premonitions seriously unless you suffer from mental health conditions.

It is common knowledge that mental health illnesses can confuse the best of us and often play tricks on our normal thought processes. I would not suggest expanding your intuitive mind if you suffer from any mental health conditions. I suggest that you delay any psychic exploration until your mind is healthy.

Our logical mind may be very suspicious of our intuition as it doubts its existence and if it does exist, why should it be trusted? We must help the human mind remember that intuitive insights are essential.

We know instinctively from birth how to work in harmony with our six senses. Many of us grow out of using our sixth sense as young children. Our parents told us that our intuitive magical experiences were just figments of our imagination. In reality, your imagination is the precursor to your intuition, which inspires you and brings out the best in you in so many ways.

Learn to access your divine connection by letting go of the need to control what you sense and feel. Mini meditations and yoga breathing are excellent ways to start. It's important to remember to balance and cleanse your energy field daily as you continue this journey. There is no doubt that your life will change as you start to take advantage of these incredible revelations. Your lifestyle will become more harmonious and you can thrive by accessing divine wisdom.

> Anne-Marie here!
>
> Just checking in on you. Are you enjoying the book? Have any questions? Make sure you join our Facebook group, scan the QR code below.
>
> You know, people sometimes ask me, "are you a medium?"... and seriously, I have to reply... "no, I'm an extra-large!"
>
> While your intuitive abilities are a serious matter, Spirit loves it when we have fun, a laugh and a joke, as it raises our vibration or frequency.
>
> Okay, back to the book, just remember you can do anything you set your mind to as long as you are having fun in the process!
>
> Anne-Marie

Join our FaceBook group

Your spiritual tool box

Take a few deep breaths to quiet your mind and introduce your rational mind to your intuitive sense, affirming that it brings beautiful insight and awareness straight from the divine. It is part of your soul that came with you into this lifetime. It wants to work in harmony with your five human senses and can enhance your life in many ways. It may sense danger or fantastic opportunities that defy any logical explanation.

Affirm now that you want to take advantage of this by saying, 'I am a divine being having a human experience and I allow divine wisdom to guide me.'

Our 'Sixth Sense' is here to help us accept vital messages. Would you discredit your hearing if you heard a siren? Would you ignore your friend who needs to talk to you? So, why would you ignore your intuition? Every time you see a sign or receive an intuitive message, tell your brain that it came from the divine. When you identify the message's source, your human brain is less likely to reject this wisdom.

Half the battle is won when you get your minds to work in harmony, when you know how you receive messages. From now on, every time you receive an intuitive message or see a sign, thank your intuition for showing you the signals and sending the messages. Tell it that you appreciate the heads up. Tell your brain thank you for not discounting this message and this will help all your senses work in harmony.

Exercise - visualize

Here is a mini visualisation that will help you make a solid bond between your brain and your intuitive mind. Please ensure that you are somewhere quiet where you will not be disturbed. Remember not to operate machinery, drive or do anything else when doing any psychic exercises or meditations.

1. Take a few deep breaths and put your right hand on your heart.
2. Breathe in deeply and slowly for five seconds mentally counting 1001, 1002, 1003, 1004 and 1005.
3. Hold for five seconds then breathe out for five seconds.
4. Do this three to five times until you feel relaxed and grounded.

5. Call upon your angels, spirit guides and lost loved ones to surround you with love as you begin to work at uniting your mind, body and soul with your spiritual mind.
6. Visualize yourself in the center of a beautiful and clear crystal ball. It extends three feet above your head, three feet down into the ground and spans three feet around you in every direction.
7. It has an exterior that is as strong as a diamond. Beams of love and light shine through, nourishing you and giving you positive white light energy and strength. Negativity runs off the exterior like rain off an umbrella.
8. The uplifting beams of love and light magnify your 6th sense connection to the divine. You notice a strong cord that flows from your belly button and reaches up into the heavens, transmitting positive energy.

All the rainbow colors fill your crystal ball along with love and healing. Visualize Archangel Gabriel standing just outside your crystal ball.

My prayers often change but usually resemble something like this.

"Thank you Archangel Gabriel for working with me daily. I am grateful for your help in expanding my psychic abilities and connection to the divine. I graciously accept, acknowledge and receive messages from Spirit. And so it is. Amen."

If you have chosen a card as your focal point for your meditation, start staring at the card you selected and see what comes to you while focusing on what this card means. My prayer is only a suggestion and the interpretation conveyed to you is the one you should adopt. When finished, thank the Infinite Spirit and Archangel Gabriel for their protection, wisdom and guidance. Repeat this exercise daily until you are comfortable with it. You may find that you adapt it slightly to suit yourself in time.

Remember to make notes about this exercise, opposite.

Did you see anything, hear or sense anything? Did anything resonate with you or give you an a-ha moment?

More ways to connect

Have you ever had a light bulb moment while taking a shower, cleaning the windows or washing the dishes?

There are many ways to connect with your higher self and Spirit but not all ways work for all people. The main ingredient for getting into the zone is putting your conscious thoughts to the back of your mind. During this time, while you are thinking about nothing, you are in the Alpha state of mind or what some would call meditation.

When you are in the Alpha state of mind or the meditation state you can tap into your innate abilities, plug into your intuition and experience the magic of being in the zone.

You do not have to meditate in the traditional ways with legs crossed and saying ohms, in fact traditional meditation often puts me to sleep. You'll find a few of my favorite ways to connect with Spirit in the following pages. If one does not work for you then try a different method.

Singing and dancing

One of my favourite ways to calm and clear my mind is by doing a moving meditation. It is quick, easy and simple to do.

The purpose is to raise your vibration and chase away any intrusive thoughts and feelings that seem to be getting in your way. It is impossible to think or feel negative thoughts while dancing and singing along to upbeat music. It dissolves your negative energy blockage automatically. Turn on the music and sing and dance to some of your favourite happy songs for 10 to 20 minutes, I have a few different play list on YouTube that I use depending on my mood.

When you need to quieten your mind because you feel frustrated or angry, sing along with and dance to two or three upbeat songs and then switch the tempo down a little by moving slower to two or three of your favourite, gentle uplifting tunes. It will help you achieve the right frame of mind and helps you become more centered and balanced.

Music changes the vibration you resonate with far quicker than anything else. It can help you start your psychic exploration work and is always an excellent way to start your day!

It will help you smile and leave your worries in the wind.

Candles and journaling

Sometimes your mind will just not shut up, it may be all over the place when all you want is to focus. Another way of tuning out intrusive thoughts is to sit somewhere quietly.

Get your notepad and write a list of the things running around in your head. Leave a couple of spaces after each one so you have room to write your solutions. Look at your list and decide which of these issues can be solved quickly and which will take a little more time.

Next, put numbers beside each item in the order you want to tackle them. When you cannot fix something today, write it down and make the conscious decision to let it wait until the divine has decided it is the right time. This practice helps calm your mind so you can get into the zone.

Your mind will categorize what is important and prioritize what you need to do. It will dismiss any random intrusive thoughts that are not helpful and file away your worries for another time until you can do something about them.

Now you have a plan

Light a candle, even a tea light will do, take some deep breaths and stare at the flame for approximately five minutes. Blow out the candle and shuffle your cards while asking: What will the day bring?

Look carefully at the images and say out loud what comes to your mind. They could tell you several things or give an overall theme for the day. Sometimes, they can warn that your day may not progress as planned. You can adjust your frame of mind or change your schedule to see if you can get your day to go more smoothly than the card indicated. Later in the evening, look back on your card message to see how it related to your day. When you do this daily, it will help you gain more insight into the meaning of your cards and the way you interpret them.

Grounding meditation

You might need grounding, use this exercise when you have settled down a little but are still not yet in the zone. Sit quietly, close your eyes and take a few deep breaths. Imagine there is a cord attached to the base of your spine, this cord goes down through the floor and deep into the earth. Think of it like a tree root being grounded and nourished by mother earth. We call this a grounding cord.

Next, visualize a bright, beautiful light traveling up the cord. It is coming through the soles of your feet and filling every part of your body with the most brilliant light containing love, compassion and healing. Your negative emotions and fearful thoughts like anger, hopelessness and pain, melt away into nothingness with this incredible healing grounding energy.

Then see a similar bright light coming to you from the divine. It enters your head via your crown chakra and fills your body with the highest, brilliant light filled with love, light, balance and harmony. See both of these lights swirl around your body in different directions, they blend and become one in a beautiful kaleidoscope of light. See this light fill every corner of your mind, body and soul. Allow the energies to become one with you. Once they seem to have settled and grounded you, open your eyes and you'll bring these beautiful blessings into your day! If you're sick, depressed or plagued by negativity, do this morning and night for a month to experience the beautiful changes it brings.

Connecting your intuition with your cards

Card decks are for divination, inspirational meditation or spiritual purposes. Tarot cards are Oracle cards too, they're different because the tarot has a set structure, while Oracle cards are more free wheeling. It is more than OK to use both tarot and Oracle cards during your readings. Each will bring you a different perspective. Once you have become good at reading one deck you can add another to bring another aspect to your car readings.

You should be able to connect well with the 6th Sense Connection Oracle cards. They trigger your intuition and get your psychic energy flowing. I enjoy working with card decks that have vivid imagery. It's said that a picture speaks a thousand words to you in different ways. That is part of the reason I chose the images I did for 6th Sense Connection Oracle cards. I was over the moon when they won the best new divination product from the coalition of original resources in 2020, It took years to carefully craft and design them.

Choose a card deck that you feel a connection with and in no time at all it will start speaking to you. You might feel a tingle when you hold them or get a strong sense that these are your new cards.

When you unwrap a deck for the first time, take a few minutes to become acquainted with the images and guidebook. Do the author's words resonate with you? Do you feel a buzz or some good energy radiating from these cards? If you do, these are the cards you should be working with for now.

To cleanse their energy and make them yours, shuffle the cards and then arrange them in numerical order. Next, take a few deep breaths, hold them to your heart say...

"Thank you for coming into my life; you are now a bridge that will help me connect my intuition with the divine. Thank you for agreeing to help me with my quest to see the signs and hear the messages. And so it is. Amen".

By doing this, you are dedicating your deck and allowing it to become one of the tools you use to make your connection to the divine.

When learning to read cards intuitively, read the guidebook that came with your cards and, refer back to it as and when needed. You might find referring back to the guidebook helpful while learning to read your new deck. Once you have looked at the layout and gained all you can from your intuition, if you still feel something more needs to come to light, refer to the guide book for a different perspective.

You will connect more with the cards and need the guidebook less when you give your intuition the attention it needs to grow and become your new best friend. Once you get to know your cards, you'll develop your meanings for each card. Be open to the fact that these meanings are not cast in stone either. Their meaning may change depending on how they look in their layout combined with the other cards in the spread. Other factors will also come into play, such as what the angels or spirit guides tell you or what you are intuitively sensing during the session.

Forming a bond with your cards may happen quickly or may take some time to click into place. Select a card and if you can, carry this card around with you during the day and look at it often. If you work at a desk, place it in clear sight and see if it speaks to you about what is happening during your day. You might find that people and situations show up that help you gain a deeper understanding of this card. It is a fun way to get to know your cards better.

It is OK to refer back to the guidebook for the definitions until you form a unique solid connection with your cards. Take one at a time and look at the images on each card carefully. Do they remind you of someone or a particular situation? Your card is talking to you intuitively and the synchronicity in this relationship has begun to blossom! Try not to get over-excited or you will slip out of the zone and revert to thinking and figuring out how this happened.

Take some deep, slow breaths and see if you can quickly get back into the zone. If you do not get back into your intuitive mind quickly, try again later or the next day if you are determined not to let your logical mind get in the way. Alternatively, do the grounding meditation and unless you are too tired, this will work perfectly.

Take the same card to bed with you and place it under your pillow while you sleep. You may be pleasantly surprised with a dream about the card. Prophetic dreams are straightforward, uncanny and often very inspiring. If you decide to study your cards this way, ensure to keep a journal on your bedside cabinet to write everything down as soon as you wake up. You may have fascinating dreams that are straightforward and not discombobulated. Write what you sensed, saw or felt, as this could be part of your unique connection with the card and the divine.

Bear in mind that there are no rules for what the cards mean. They mean what you believe they mean to you. Once you forge a deeper bond with them, you will arrive at your unique meaning or variations of the ones that came with your guidebook. If nothing new comes to mind, then the author's meaning stands for the time being. Once you have worked through the deck, you can start again at your discretion or allow Spirit to lead you while reading your cards.

Part 3

Readings

The goal of any intuitive psychic reading is to gain insight and to be inspired by the messages received. We all need something positive to look forward to, happier times or better days are always welcome.

When reading for others and if the reading talks about some difficulty that the person has to overcome, ensure you look for things that will give them hope for the future. Reassurance that good times are on their way once this struggling phase is over will uplift and inspire them. It will help them focus on the positive things coming their way. Readings should be helpful, informative and help navigate challenging situations as efficiently as possible. Think of it as a glimpse into what can be. While some life situations may be difficult to avoid, we can choose how we react to them. Using the cards can bring insights that may help you make the best of any situation.

If you ask essential questions differently, you will gain insight into how a situation may be approached differently and result in a more desirable outcome. You can ask your cards for suggestions on how you can tweak things. Hence, you will find ideas and tips on how this situation can be turned around to minimize adverse effects.

The future is not cast in stone and we are masters of our destiny. We all have some divine appointments or pre-life challenges to 'grow through' during our lifetime. These challenges are predetermined and we rarely get advance knowledge of them. Sometimes, it feels like a tornado has touched down without any warning. We don't know what to do or where to turn. We can talk to friends and get their opinion of what they might do in our situation but the choice is ours.

When it is your situation that you need to resolve, only you can decide how to do it; what does your gut tell you? Think about consulting your cards for a different perspective of your challenge. You still have some control and can decide how you react to any situation. You can get upset and lose your temper, ignore it or take a step back, take a few deep breaths and consult your cards. You are looking for ways around the problem, to circumvent it or better yet, meeting it with strength and clarity, looking for the best step forward.

Decide how to handle the situation and, 'grow through,' it with as much grace and ease as possible. We all have free will and we can change the course of our future at any point in time. We can rise to the occasion or decide to bury our heads in the sand until we have the strength and determination to bring it to a satisfactory conclusion.

Using your cards will help you gain valuable insight into what you can do to turn things around. Think of your reading as an advance weather forecast, if you know it will rain you could wear a coat and carry an umbrella or you might postpone your trip until weather conditions are more favorable.

What you see in a psychic reading is likely to happen if you continue on your proposed course. If you decide to do things differently, the outcome may well change.

Shuffling the cards

The most important thing to remember is to silence your mind and focus on what you would like to know. I have seen people hold conversations while shuffling, often bringing mixed results to their readings with little clarity. There is no right or wrong way to shuffle or handle the cards, so do what feels right.

If a card comes out upside-down, don't automatically assume that this places a reverse meaning on the card. Ask Spirit for clarification as it may be just revealing the person's fears or yours if the reading is for you. When you have finished working with your cards, I recommend that you put them back in numerical order, as this is an excellent way of cleansing the vibes and influences of the reading. It will also help you memorize their numbers and images.

Once in a while, a card will become temporarily misplaced. Recognize that Spirit is trying to get you to pay attention to an important message. Note when and where the card is found as this could be part of the message when you find it. For example, if you misplace the 'Emerge card' and find it on the floor, it could be a message telling you to look for opportunities that are at your feet and have not yet considered? Spirit is trying to get you to look at how you can emerge into a better situation.

There are opportunities for you to take a leading role somewhere right now, which would be most beneficial to you. If nothing comes to mind or you are unaware of any opportunity at the moment, see what emerges in time.

When reading for others

I am asked a lot about who should shuffle the cards when doing a reading for someone else? There are no rules except the ones you adopt. It depends on how you feel about other people touching your cards. When you are close to other people you have entered their energy field. You decide what feels right to you, it works just as well. I know psychics who prefer to let the client shuffle and cut the cards. I know others who never let anyone else touch their cards. Some do elaborate shuffles and cuts and select the pile that stands out to them.

I usually start by letting the client shuffle the cards when doing readings in person and try to keep it simple, I believe that when clients shuffle the cards they put their energy into them. I prefer to let their hands decide where the cards need to end up rather than cutting them in a traditional game of cards. My theory is that a fancy cut flicks off the energy just put on the cards. I ask people not do a fancy bridge card shuffle and add, "We are not playing poker, we are consulting the oracle. I want your energy imprinted on the cards during the reading."

Sometimes when the questioner shuffles the cards, what you see is the opposite of what your sixth sense and guides are telling you. Always trust your gut. Ask yourself, "Is this person very nervous or fearful?" Their fear and confusion may be influencing their energy and what you see in the cards could be their fears. Tell them it is OK. What I'm sensing from Spirit is the opposite of what the cards say. It may be because you are nervous, no worries. I am not anxious and I sense good things are in store for you, let me shuffle instead. Take note of what you have seen and see if there were any similarities when you shuffled.

When I look in detail at particular areas or questions, I tend to shuffle the cards myself or ask the client to select some cards that I spread out face down.

Reading disclosures

In countries like the UK, you have to make a legal disclosure before giving clients a psychic reading. I use the phrase "Readings are for entertainment purposes only." I continue to provide that disclosure in the USA too. I don't want anyone's life to be dominated by what happens during a reading. The future has not happened yet and we all have free will. Tell them to think of their psychic reading as an advanced weather forecast. If they know it may rain, they can take an umbrella or postpone the trip for another day.

What you see during a reading is what is likely to happen if they continue doing what they intend to do. If they change their direction, they change the outcome. Be kind and compassionate when you are doing readings. People will remember what you said and the way it was delivered. Say what you feel, hear and see. Try and focus on the good things coming up while being helpful and informative.

Ask Spirit to help you provide sensitive information in a kind and compassionate way. Perhaps a potential break up in a close relationship or a career move that doesn't appear to be in their best interests. Help them see options around these situations to prepare to minimize the effects if they cannot avoid the situation altogether. The company they are working for may be closing down, so perhaps they should focus on saving up while looking for a new job.

It could be that they are in a volatile relationship and no matter what they do, they cannot seem to make this relationship loving and happy. Remember, it takes two to tango. The other party has to be willing to work on this relationship too. Be considerate, you do not want what you said to play on their mind too much! Encouragement, compassion and inspiration will be more helpful than being a negative.

If this reading is about family, you might want to encourage the client to spend more quality time with loved ones. They could be a workaholic and spend too much time at work and not enough time with family. Someone close may need to spend more quality time with them. Ask your cards more questions to gain a deeper insight and receive more clarification.

Sincere, honest advice from the cards or your own life experiences is usually welcome. If you feel someone needs professional help like counseling to heal from trauma, tell them to ask their doctor or friends for a referral. Everything you tell them must be completely confidential. Trust plays a vital part between reader and client. If you are genuine and sincere and give them honest and caring consultations, they will come back for more.

Preparing to do readings

When doing psychic readings you are channeling spiritual energy. You need to feel fit and healthy and put anything that has been upsetting you to one side. Especially if you are worried about something happening in your life, information about your issues might come through during your client's reading. And that is not good for the client. If you are physically or emotionally unwell and you have readings scheduled, it would be better to ask your clients to reschedule. During illness your energy will be weaker and your connection to the divine might not be as clear and strong.

It does not matter if you are reading remotely via video or phone or in the same room. As the channeler, it takes a lot of energy from you to bring forward clear and concise messages that your clients need to hear. Spirit often steps in for me before I have a chance to ask someone to reschedule, clients often contact me first to let me know that something has come up and they need to reschedule. I tend to think that Spirit is looking out for both of us and everything happens with divine timing.

Readings done via video chat are just as good as those done in person. You will feel like you are in the same room with the person as long as you make a good connection. I do mine via zoom and ask the client if they want their session recorded and email it to them later.

Some clients like to watch the session again, while others have committed it to memory. Once in a while, a client does not want their session recorded. It is all about the client and what they want to take from their session while keeping their reading private.

Once in a while, the recording will fail, so I do not guarantee that they will receive a recording of the session. It is in the hands of Spirit; if they are supposed to get the recording, they will!

When you are ready to do readings, it is time to tap into some beautiful, uplifting energy; think of it as going to meet someone special.

How to prepare

Prepare by allowing at least ten minutes ahead of your reading to get yourself relaxed and in the zone. I prepare in my office, which I dedicate to my spiritual work, it is my sacred space! I like to play inspirational music softly in the background. There are lots of crystals and all kinds of mystical treasures that I have collected over the years. I may burn some incense or light a candle as I meditate.

When you are ready to read the cards, take a few deep breaths to quiet your mind. Breathe in slowly for five seconds (Do this by counting 1001, 1002, 1003, 1004, 1005), hold for five seconds breathe out for five seconds. Do this five times. Next, ask your angels, spirit guides and lost loved ones for spiritual protection while you connect. Imagine yourself inside a massive crystal ball. It has a surface as hard as diamond. It allows uplifting light energy to shine in but it reflects darker negativity outward and away from the safe space surrounding your energy field and crystal ball.

If you sense any negative or heavy energy, the best place to send it is into the ground where mother nature can make good use of it by recycling it. Think of it as giving back and feeding the earth. The uplifting energies feel warm and magnify your 6th sense connection with the divine. If you allow in negative energy by mistake, it will zap your energy and leave you feeling tired and drained.

Call upon your angels by saying...

Calling all guardian angels, spirit guides, lost loved ones, ancestors, ascended masters and those of whom look out for (state the name of the person you are reading for). Please join us and share your wisdom, insights and anything else you think (name your client) needs to know.

Next, see yourself in a huge and beautiful library in the most wonderful, heavenly place. Instinctively go to the section of the library where your client's book of life is stored. Visualize yourself taking it down from the shelf and opening it up to gain deeper insights and information regarding this person. Ask your client's permission to consult the Akashic records on their behalf.

Ask them to relax and clear their mind and take a few deep breaths with you while you are connecting with their Spirit guides and angels, the Akashic records and lost loved ones. It will help them relax and open up their energy field so you can pick up more informative information for them.

Remember to ask their permission to step into their energy field. Doing this helps you receive more information about them and what they need to know. Tell them you will not be able to see everything, only what they want you to see. Tell them if you speak about anything that they feel uncomfortable discussing, they can ask you to stop at any time and focus on something different. When they want a general reading, try and leave five to ten minutes at the end of the session to answer any questions.

During a reading

Think about recording your sessions on video or audio. Say what you sense, hear, feel, smell or see with your third eye, often referred to as second sight. You will feel very relaxed in a slightly altered state of awareness, known as an 'alpha state of mind', which allows us to be calm, focused and receptive. We can tap into spiritual information in this state of awareness and become more resourceful and open to our intuitive connection to the divine.

If you start having conversations while in the zone, you'll slip out of your relaxed state of mind, become lively and end up back in your rational mind. When you try to rationalize or analyze what the cards mean, you will also slip out of the zone. You need to be in harmony with Spirit and listen to the messages that come to you with an open mind. It might not make sense to you but say it anyway. What is coming through is not about you, it is about your client. They should understand what Spirit is saying. They may get an a-ha moment now or later when they have time to reflect on what was said. Sometimes, they are nervous or overexcited, so take a moment and try and help them relax. The reading will progress more smoothly when your client feels centerd and calm.

Next, decide what spread you will use, shuffle the cards while focusing on the question you would like to know more about and stop when they feel ready. A good question would be, "What does Spirit want me to know about this person?"

When you have the answer, ask other questions, look into different areas of their life, relationships, home, family or career. You'll be surprised at what you can see and how helpful the reading is for them.

Practice with friends and family and you will be amazed at how valuable and relevant the information is for them.

When reading for yourself, an excellent place to start would be to ask, "What will the day bring?" Note what happens during the day and refer to your notes at the end of the day.

Here are my observations of the card that I drew for today. When you pull a card like Union for the day's theme, your first reaction might be, why did this card come up? I stared at it and did not seem to receive much spiritual insight, I guess I had slipped out of the zone while wondering how this card would unfold during my day. It was a Saturday, so I did not think any business would be going on. I put it to one side and came back to it later.

Next, I opened Facebook to find a memory that one of my best friends posted, about a night out we had in Orlando five years ago. We went to a nightclub, met up with other friends and danced a lot! We celebrated our sis-starhood and the union of good friends. One of them is my sister from another mother and although we live far apart now, we are never far from each other's hearts and minds.

Then my partner and I spent time preparing our suitcases for our upcoming vacation. Later we went shopping to buy some last-minute items we needed for our trip. On the way back, we dropped in to see my parents. We finished packing the suitcases together and loaded up the car! Cleaned house, even though it was clean, I have to go through my routine of cleaning everything before we go on vacation. Then settled down together for a cozy evening and an early night. So, even though I doubted it, the day's card was spot on about what would happen in my day!

When reading for someone else and you would like to know something about them ahead of time, a good question to ask is, How does this person see themselves? The card pulled was for example, Free Spirit

When you read for them, decide if they look like they have a free spirit and march to the beat of their drum? Perhaps, the intuitive message you are receiving is, They need to get back to being themselves and quit worrying about what other people say or think about them. It is time they decided it is OK to be unique and own their eccentricities. Should this person be on a spiritual path and be able to embrace their divine essence?

Ask them whether they see angels in the clouds. If not, tell them to look up and embrace the world's wonders! All kinds of magical and

2. Free Spirit

mystical things are waiting to play a role in their lives. They might need to expand their circle and meet other like-minded people. They may feel stifled in their current relationship or perhaps something happened that makes them think they have to hide their unique nature. When you read for this person, ask questions like "What does this person need to know to become more authentic to themselves?"

Explore this with them and help them see how they can improve their lives. Another question to ask would be, "Does this person live in an environment that encourages them to be all they can be?"

Sadly, some people live in situations where spiritual expression is limited by their religious beliefs, prohibiting any psychic spiritual exploration. Others may live in an atmosphere where it is frowned upon to be different, so they go along to get along. Your client may be happy in this environment, as they feel safe within these strict boundaries. Encourage them to make small changes over time and they should meet less resistance. The message here is that they can compromise if they do not sacrifice their divine essence. Their partner or loved ones should appreciate and acknowledge this by giving this person space to be themselves.

When laying the cards out during general readings, look at each card carefully and then look at them as an unfolding story. What is the theme this reading is taking? What are the first things that come to mind? Ask the client if they can relate to what is coming through during the session. You might be surprised to see how the theme of the reading connects directly with your client's life. Will it be about the person and how they can prosper and be happy with their life? Are there any issues that must be acknowledged, accepted released to make the most of the present? Are they too busy looking at what is wrong instead of focusing on what is right with their lives? Too many people go through life beating themselves up over things that happened that were beyond their control.

You can help them see that it was one of those situations that they needed to grow through. Perhaps they approached this situation with good intentions and were deceived by others? Help them see that other people and factors contributed to this situation. Ask the cards more questions to shed light on the lesson. It will stop your client from thinking that they should have done things differently.

If your mind wanders or you end up speaking during the process, stop and start again. Some people continue while being distracted, which will cause the reading to become confused. Remember, you cannot shuffle the cards and stay in the zone while talking.

Akashic record readings

When you want insight into the near future, use a spread like the 'Celtic Cross.' It shows you what is happening and how things are changing on the current path. It details what will be going on and how it can affect home, family and future trends. When we use divination, we are looking into 'The Akashic Records', known as the library of the Divine. Everyone's book of life is stored here and can be read by those who have consent.

Think of it as the Google of the divine, where you can access information about a person, place or situation. Imagine entering this impressive library and opening the book of the person who has asked you for the reading. You may only open the book of records for another person as long as you have their permission. Otherwise, you are being nosey. It is like trespassing on private property and just like nosy neighbors, you may not be able to see things correctly.

It is unethical to attempt to read for someone without their consent. For example, when someone wants to know if their ex will come back, you will be allowed to look into this briefly. The purpose of the sneaky peek is for the greater good of the person you are helping. More often than not, the answer will allow them to move on and leave the past behind.

You will not be able to see what is happening in-depth with their ex. You should be able to see if the ex is happy with life now. I tend to shy away from these readings unless the person requesting it is ready to accept the answer. Ninety-nine percent of the time, not letting go of an ex-lover will block the person from making the most of their life. When someone is grieving for an old lover to come back to them, ask the cards, "Why did this relationship fail?"

Did it have a chance to become a successful relationship? Some relationships are like fireworks, glowing and sparkling and then they fizzle out. Ask the client to consider this relationship is over and the feeling is no longer mutual. They may be in love with a dream of what they could have become together.

Perhaps this person was not as good for them as they remember. I ask the client to think about this relationship and how this person treated them. Possibly, the energies did not blend as well as they thought.

The big question that helps many people get their a-ha moment is: Would you be happy with your child dating and marrying this person?

More often than not, the answer is no. Then I add, if this person is not good enough for them, they are not good enough for you. It is time to find someone who loves you and makes you an essential part of their life.

If they are in an unhealthy relationship, you should be able to see some of the issues. Try and gain some insight on what they can do to improve the relationship or perhaps it is better for them to walk away? Remember, what you see is likely to happen if they stay on the current course. If they tweak things in some way, they can usually change the outcome.

It is like asking Google maps for directions to take you to London but you decide you want to stop at Stonehenge along the way. You may travel on some of the same roads but the experience will be different. It is always good to look into choices and options for the best advice.

When reading for yourself, avoid slipping out of the zone and into your logical mind. When this happens start over again.

Don't get distracted by writing down your observations during your session. A better idea is to record it, saying aloud what you sense, see, hear or feel during the session. You might get some fascinating insight and this is an excellent way to get to know your cards and how they work with you.

Reverse card meanings

Some readers like to use reverse card meanings, it is a personal preference and you either feel driven to read them reversed or decide to place them the right way up. Once you have established your intuitive relationship with your cards, remember to use it when you see a card reversed. The bond you establish with them will determine if you will see a lot of reversals. I do not pay much attention to reverse cards unless it seems crucial to the overall theme.

Once I have laid the spread out and gained an overall impression, I decide if there is a reversed card that needs to stay that way. I look at the cards more when the odd one shows up. There are plenty of cards that can tell the story they need to tell without appearing to be upside down. If there are quite a few reversals in a spread, it could be the person's insecurities or fears that have surfaced.

Sometimes, the surrounding cards support the meaning of the reversed card and the reading makes more sense that way. At other times it can feel like the elephant in the room; we decide if it needs some attention or if we ignore it as it makes no sense when considered in context with the surroundings.

Reading any reversed card is exactly that; it means the opposite of the card's meaning if it were the right-way up. For example, if the 'Procrastination Card' shows up reversed in a reading, it can indicate the person is perhaps being too hasty and they should look before they leap.

Alternatively, it could mean that they are in the right place at the right time and on the fast track to success. The accompanying cards in the spread should show you an accurate picture of the events and how they are unfolding.

When the connection becomes cloudy

Avoid chatting during the reading or you may lose your intuitive connection. You will begin to revert to the cards' guidebook meaning and slip out of reading intuitively. Some readers go by logic and there is nothing wrong with using the author's interpretations however, you will gain more knowledgeable insight by staying in your intuitive energy.

You can chat later, ask for quiet time so you can tap back into the divine, take a few deep breaths and quiet your mind. Ask your spirit guides, angels and lost loved ones to help you keep out of your rational mind.

You need to be in your intuitive mind and affirm that you will only allow information to flow from the divine. Become completely relaxed so that you can make a strong connection.

Remember, your cards work like a window to glimpse potential scenarios. They are also like a bridge that helps you connect with the divine and show you what's going on. You have slipped out of the zone when trying to rationalize what the cards mean.

If you are not connecting

Once in a while you might not be able to connect with someone, the energies do not blend well with yours at all. It is not the end of the world and nothing terrible will happen to them.

Close the session

It's no use trying to do a reading when you are not connecting with their energies or guides. Recommend they see another reader, refund any fees charged, wish them well and ask the angels to bless them.

Don't take it personally and don't let your ego get in the way by telling them they are blocking you. Something could be going on that you are not allowed to see, as this could influence their choices too much Spirit prefers them not to get advice or help from you.

When your reading is complete

Once you have finished connecting, you will need to do a closing prayer or affirmation. This applies to anyone including yourself, that you've been reading. Try using something like this...

"I thank the spirits, angels and guides that shared this great information with me today. I am grateful for your wisdom, love guidance." (Take your time with this part).

"I see and feel the cleansing white light descending around and upon my energy field, cleansing and revitalizing my energy from the top of my head to my toes. I feel my body grounded to mother earth and so it is, Amen."

Wash your hands and shake your arms and hands as a symbolic gesture that you are cleaning yourself and clearing the energy from the reading. In essence, you will develop over time what works best for you.

Do not forget these steps; Prepare, Open, Read and Close

When you forget to close the reading properly, it can be like this; imaging driving a car on a journey and when you return home, you leave the car with the engine running in the driveway. It would not be suitable for the car, would it? It's not ideal for the body either, that's why I strongly recommend that you close down the reading properly.

Strengthening your intuitive connection

When you start doing readings and you want to strengthen your intuitive connection with the divine, ask spirit questions that may be helpful on your path.

Such as "What does Spirit want me to know about my intuition?"

The answer will show you what you need to do to make the most of it. You may need a little help or it could be precisely where you need it to be right now.

We are all constantly changing and the cards will tell you where your focus should be to help encourage your abilities. If the cards look like you are sprinkled with pixie dust and filled with intuitive psychic abilities already, that is awesome. They can reveal all kinds of things to you.

Use the basic three-card spread* for this question unless you sense that you should use a more extensive card spread.

*The three card spread and instructions on page 67.

I asked the question...
"What does Spirit want me to know about my intuition?"

Use the cards as a focal point and see what pops into your intuitive mind. Here is my take on this reading.

Answer
Card 1 the background
Cut the Cords

Remember to cut the cords daily, especially after reading or encountering someone or something that drains your energy. Doing this will eliminate the after-effects of being in someone else's energy. Your thoughts and feelings about them and any negative thoughts and feelings about yourself need to go too. The energy attached to you during your encounter needs to be grounded. Doing this cord-cutting cleansing will encourage a stronger connection to your intuition.

I sometimes forget to cut the cords after speaking with people. As a psychic empath, I tend to draw away the negative energy from the people I work with, which is a bonus for them. People often tell me they feel better when they have spoken with me. Readings can be very healing as well as informative. When your heart reaches out to someone during any heartfelt conversation as an empath, you naturally draw away from them their negative energies. I also need to remember to have my shields up and strengthened during conversations.

Answer
Card 2 Present Conditions
Soul Mate

My intuition is a part of my divine essence and my first 'Soul Mate.' It came with me into this lifetime to help me every step of the way. I need to spend time with it daily so that we may communicate with each other. We can work together and talk to each other throughout our day, especially during our daily meditations. Often, answers to questions or solutions to problems pop into our minds. Sometimes this happens when we are in our quiet space and our minds are open to communication with our intuition.

It is nice to say thank you to your intuitive connection for the insights it shares. Tell it you enjoy having it as a part of your life. It speaks to us in so many ways throughout the day.

Watch for the signs it sends you, not only in the cards but at other times in your everyday world. Our intuitive connection brings magic into our world and enriches our lives beyond belief. It will never let us down, it has been our constant companion from birth and will leave this planet with us when we cross over.

Answer
Card 3 Outcome
Knight

This card tells us that our intuition's job is to be our knight in shining armor and come to our rescue no matter the situation we have gotten ourselves mixed up in. It does not shy away from anything and will help defend and protect us to the end of our lifetime. Imagine having such a trusted ally. It is your best friend in the world!

As long as you forge deep and strong bonds with it, you will hear the messages it sends.

Remember to let it know that you have listened to the message and not discarded it. You might not understand why it tells you something about a person, place or situation, but it will become apparent in time. Acknowledge that it knows things before you do. It will keep you safe and on track as long as you pay attention to what it shares.

Your knight is your light-bringer and fights for goodness and mercy to be with you always. It knows better than any other being about your prospects and the best way for you to handle any situation. There is no better person to have your back.

Caring for your cards

My cards seem to tell me how they would like to be stored when I am not using them. I store some of my card decks in their original packaging. I put others into lovely velvet drawstring bags with a crystal or two or a decorative wooden box along with sage and crystals.

I sort them out numerically after each reading. It is my way of cleansing and removing the vibrations or energy of the previous client. I inherited this practice from my mother. She feels that if she did not do this after each client; she would be trying to start a new reading on top of an old one. It frequently happened when she had a lot of clients scheduled on the same day.

Think about using two or three decks and switch them between each client so the cards' energy can rest and re-set. Otherwise your readings may look the same as the previous one. Take a few decks with you when reading in a public space, where many people may be around you.

Once in a while, a card will become misplaced and when this happens it's a message for you! What has Spirit been trying to get you to look at in your own life? Thank Spirit for the heads up. Then look around the room and on the floor again.

Please pay special attention to where you find it. If it is on the floor, perhaps this energy needs to be either grounded or transformed in your life. If it turns up in between cards in the wrong place after you have sorted your cards in numerical order, consider the energy of cards on either side of the one you found, as this is a three-card message. Not everyone is familiar with sorting their cards out into numerical order.

Some psychics place a cleansing crystal on their cards and wrap their cards in silk. Others place them back into the box they came in or put them in a dedicated decorative wooden box.

My mother sorts hers out and then puts her cards on her decorative bowl filled with tumbled stones and crystals on her reading room desk. I recommend that you do what feels right for you. If you are not sure, sort them out as I do for now. In time, you will come up with a ritual that works for you.

Retiring your cards

Sadly, your older deck needs to be retired when the images fade and the backs of the cards reveal tell-tale marks of their identity. They have served you well and have given you many insights to help others. I am very respectful of the way I dispose of my old cards. I do a meditation with them and thank them for their service and help. I put them to one side for a while as sometimes resting them will help them rejuvenate.

Once it is clear that they need to be retired permanently, I burn them outdoors with some sage while saying a little prayer to thank them for their blessings and excellent insights. I sprinkle their ashes in my flower garden. If you enjoy working with a particular card deck, ensure you have a replacement deck on hand. I tend to work with two sets and switch them between clients on busier days, so they get to rest and reset properly.

One of my older sis-star psychics, Philimenia, used the same deck for more than twenty years. She loved the faded and worn-out images on her tattered cards. She never let anyone else touch her cards. I offered to replace them for her as a gift several times. I searched on the internet and found the deck she had so lovingly used for years. She refused my assistance and said she would not know what the new ones meant even though they looked the same.

She had built a strong relationship with this particular deck and never used any different ones. I asked her if she had ever studied their meaning in a book or taken a course?

She said "I read a book about my cards years ago. Then developed my intuitive card meanings and gave the book away". She explained that this card deck connected her to her clients' angels, spirit guides and the divine when she was doing readings.

That was her belief, so I respected her ways and never asked to replace her deck again. My ways are different from hers and yours may be different again.

Do what your intuitive mind tells you is right for you.

Obtaining cards

In this day and age, I firmly believe that if you are meant to read cards you will find yourself in places where there are cards present.

It used to be taboo to purchase cards for yourself but if you are meant to read the cards you will read the cards. The cards that are meant for you will find you.

In my case, my mother, who is also a psychic, would not gift me cards in my early twenties because she felt my imagination would run wild and I would see things that I wasn't meant to see.

Since my mother would not gift me cards, I made my own set of cards in 1982 as an experiment. Unable to afford card stock at the time, I crafted the Major Arcana of the tarot from a couple of old giant soap powder boxes. Having successfully repurposed the cardboard, I painstakingly drew the images with a marker pen. I lack artistic skills, so they were far from a work of art.

To my amazement, these poorly hand crafted cards became a window in connecting me with my sixth sense and divine inspiration. Their readings were filled with wonderfully inspired insights into relationships, families and future trends.

Part 4

Questions and card spreads

Phrasing questions

When you ask a question, you naturally expect an answer. The phrasing of your question is important and must be clear and concise to obtain a good response. Keep your question as simple as possible. When your inquiry is vague or complicated, your responses will be bizarre and confusing. Avoid using words like why, should or any word that implies doubt.

One question leads to another

Sometimes when we ask a question, the answer implies that we need to ask another question. The question may be complicated and we need to uncover more information to gain an informed response. Seeing the bigger picture will help us understand what we can do. Do not ask questions when you are not ready to hear the answers. The cards will show you insightful information that perhaps you had not considered. They help us connect the dots between what we know and what we need to know.

They show you what is going on regarding a situation, person or opportunity—sharing a fresh perspective and ideas that your spiritual mind already knows but might not be apparent or clear to you.

They will reveal an unfolding story of what will happen if you proceed on the path of the question you asked. Tarot and oracle cards are not designed to give legal or medical advice. You can use the cards to brainstorm and look for clues on making the best of a situation.

Here are a few ideas for asking questions and getting more in-depth answers. You will get the idea of how to phrase the questions from the examples on the next page. You can tweak them to suit you in various ways.

Example questions

Questions about your career

What type of career suits me best?
Is it wise for me to accept the job offer and work for X company?
What can I do to improve my financial situation?
What will happen if I continue working for my present employer?
Is it wise to change my job now?
What stands in the way of my financial success?

General questions

What will the day bring?
What opportunities are next on my path?
How do I align my spiritual path with my everyday world?
How can I navigate through this situation successfully?
What am I to learn from this situation?
How can I stop sabotaging myself?
What can I do to stay on my path?
What will the next few months bring?
How can I bring more happiness into my life?

Questions about love

What blocks me from finding true love?
How do I remove the blockages that prevent me from finding love?
What can I do to improve my relationship with (my parent, spouse, child, friend, etc.)?
What issue must I release to move on from the failed relationship?
What can I do to attract the right partner that aligns perfectly with me?

What was the lesson to learn from the failed relationship?
Is it time to find a new romantic life partner?
What is happening in my love life right now?
Is it wise to continue building a romantic relationship with this person?
What can I do to build a happier relationship?
What steps must I take to heal from the previous relationship?

When to use card spreads

There are all kinds of card spreads some have complicated layouts that you will need to refer to the book to ensure you get the format precise. I rarely use complicated spreads. Use the three, five or six-card spreads or the Celtic Cross spread to give deeper insight into your questions.

When I think about the layout, it tends to knock me out of the zone. I use classic spreads that I have used for years and know like the back of my hand. You should use card spreads that you find easy to lay out and learn. It helps you understand what the cards are telling you without rational thoughts getting in the way.

When you are starting, pulling one card for the day works well and when you want to know more, try the versatile three-card spread. It is a timeless classic that will give you a deeper insight into any question. Remember to ask the question clearly to get a good answer.

The three card spread

The first card represents the past or the background related to your query. It may show you a different perspective than the one you had imagined. However, please note that you cannot change the past or what is going on in the background. It shows you any blockages or if the conditions are favorable to move forward.

The second card will help you see the energy that this course of action may bring and if the present conditions are favorable to move forward with this proposed idea. It may show you the opportunities or challenges that need to be solved to get your desired outcome.

The third card is the result or future trend. What direction will this be taking you, closer to your goal or further away? If the third card is not positive, you can decide not to proceed or try a different approach to the question.

Think about your question and see if you can ask it differently. If the outcome still does not look favorable, think about giving this idea a miss for now.

You can always consider it later, but for now, your cards are saying it is not in your best interest to pursue this course of action. You could always do a five-card or a six-card spread with the wild card to see more in-depth answers. Some of us want to know why we should not proceed with our proposed course of action and how it will complicate our lives if we do it anyway. It is OK to ask these types of questions to gain further clarification.

Consider taking a photo of your answers and slipping them into your journal to refer back to them later, especially when you want to ask the same question again. Time may have passed by enough for you to consider this question again but the answer may be the same.

One thing is for sure, the cards never lie. When you are in the zone, you might not like the answer but it will be accurate. If you are still determined to be correct, try asking the same question again. You will probably get a slightly different perspective with different cards but your answer will show the same result.

The five-card spread

The five-card spread is one to use when you want a deeper insight into how your proposed path or question will affect your life. It will show you things you might not have thought about, so this spread is a must when considering taking action and going ahead with your proposed path. It is an extension of a three-card spread you place card four above card two and card five below card two without reshuffling.

All you need to do is select the following two cards from the top of the deck or choose any two cards that are face down from the deck that call out to you. This expansion of your reading will magnify how your proposed path will affect your everyday world and your spiritual wellbeing. Will it complicate your life or enrich it? Find out with these simple steps?

The first card represents the past or the background related to your query. It may show you a different perspective than the one you had imagined. We cannot change the past or what is happening in the background related to this situation. This card will help you gain a deeper insight into what energy has been brought to the table. It will show you the blockages or if the conditions are favorable to move forward.

The second card will help you see the energy that this brings and if the present conditions are favorable to move forward with this proposed idea. It may show you the opportunities and challenges that need to be welcome or resolved to get your desired outcome.

The third card is the result of a future trend. What direction will this be taking you, closer to your goal or further away? If the third card is not favorable, you can decide not to proceed or try a different approach to the question.

The fourth card placed above the second card, conveys advice from the spiritual realm on how this would affect you spiritually. Please take this seriously as some things may be suitable for our everyday world but do not feed our spirit. For instance, if the question is about a job offer. It may put food on the table, but perhaps we should look for another job where we could be happier.

The fifth card placed below the second card, is the advice about how this idea could affect your everyday world. For example, will this new job steal your joy? Is it too demanding on your health and wellbeing? When you look at the overall picture that the cards convey and consider them individually, your answer should be clear.

This spread offers a different perspective on the outcome should you decide to proceed. When I work with this spread, I'm often surprised by an outcome I hadn't considered. All kinds of things that you may not have thought about will reveal themselves, helping you decide.

Ask typical questions to get to know this spread and how to work with it such as...

Will working at this company be good for me?

What will happen if I pursue a romantic relationship with this person?

What is happening in my relationship with this person?

Six-card spread with a wild card

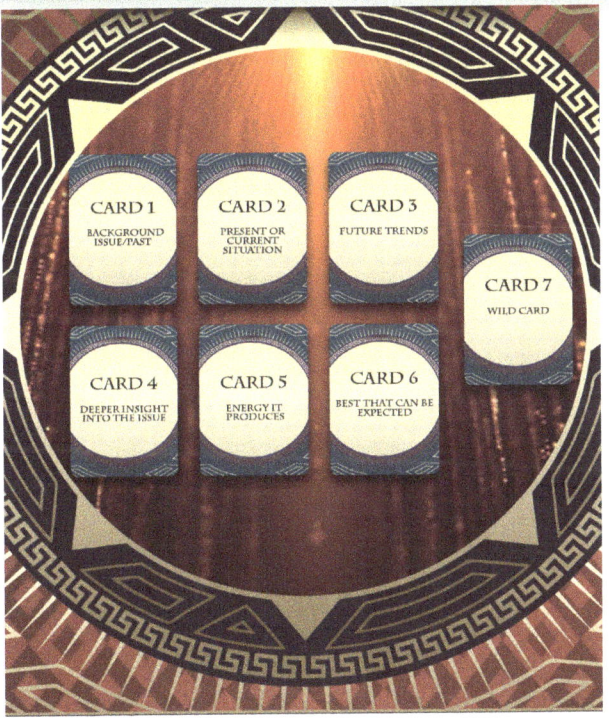

The six-card spread expands the three-card layout. It provides helpful information about your question, the actions you should or should not take and the result it could bring. Use this spread when you need more insight into the question and what action to take to achieve your desired outcome.

The first card represents the past or the background related to your query. It may show you a different perspective than the one you had imagined. However, please note that you cannot change the past or what is going on in the background. It shows you any blockages or if the conditions are favorable to move forward.

The second card will help you see the energy that this brings and if the present conditions are favorable to move forward with this proposed idea. It may show you the opportunities and challenges you need to welcome or resolve to get your desired outcome.

The third card is the result or future trend. What direction will this be taking you, closer to your goal or further away? If the third card is not favorable, you can decide not to proceed or try a different approach to the question.

Next, select four more cards from the top of the deck.

The fourth card provides a deeper insight into the issue or the background related to this situation.

The fifth card reveals more insight into the present energy it produces.

The sixth card shows you more details about the best-expected outcome or result.

The seventh card is the wild card. It shows you a different perspective. It reveals a message from Spirit about unforeseen warnings, complications, blessings, help or advice that you should consider before proceeding. If the wild card does not support your desired outcome, ask the question differently or decide not to proceed with this course of action.

Types of questions to ask to understand how this spread can work to your advantage.

- What will happen if I continue working for the same company?
- What will happen when I choose to become self-employed?
- Is it time for me to learn how to put myself first?
- Is it wise for me to pursue a friendship with this person?
- Can I become an excellent spirit medium?
- Is it wise to go on vacation with X?
- What will happen in the love affair between these two people

The year-ahead spread

The one to use for a yearly forecast. Remember, when you change your direction, you will also be changing what is coming up for you next year. If you like what you see, that's fantastic! If you would like different energy in the year, be prepared to make some positive changes that are more beneficial for you. Repeat this spread every few months to see if you are still on track or if changes are required to make to make the most of your year.

Shuffle the cards and the first card you lay out will represent the current month. The second card will be the following month so on. Once you have laid out 12 cards, the 13th card will represent you and what you need to know about the year's events and how they will affect you.

You can repeat the process by laying card number 14 over card 1, giving a deeper insight into the current month continue to card 26. You can even expand the yearly spread to a 39-card layout.

The Celtic Cross

1. Current energy or situation
2. Immediate influences coming in
3. Short term outcome
4. The past related to this question or person
5. Influences and energy that have been recently resolved or overcome
6. Your future position on the current proposed path
7. How these events affect you personally
8. How this will affect your family or home environment
9. The hidden blessings or problems on this path
10. Where this path leads and how it may affect you in the long run.

This is my version but there are several alternatives out there. If the version you like to work with differs from mine and you are happy with it, use yours! You can ask a specific question to get a more in-depth answer to an important issue or opportunity. For general readings, ask questions like: "What will the next few months bring?"

It is a versatile spread and you can use it when asking questions about relationships. For instance, Is there a long-term romantic relationship between X and Y? Would a long-term romantic relationship with Y be good for X?

Is it wise for X and Y to get divorced? Is it wise for X and Y to work on their issues and fix their relationship?

By using this spread, you will see how this path would benefit you in the long term or get in your way. You can ask any question that would significantly affect your life.

Questions you would like to have answered

Exercise - Using the previous examples, take a moment to create your own questions.

Part 5

"Life happens while we make other plans"
John Lennon

On this adventure called life, I discovered things do not always turn out the way we hoped. As disappointing as that may seem, what is important to remember is that our circumstances do not define us, nor does it mean that we have to settle for what we have achieved so far. There will always be something going on in life that wants to pull us down or hold us back. Bad things happen to good people and sadly, some challenges are hard to overcome. The life we want starts to emerge when we journey through good and bad times with love in our hearts and with an attitude of gratitude. Keep your plans flexible and fill them with your hopes and dreams.

It can be hard to keep smiling when the tide has turned against you. You can get to the core of most things and minimize their adverse effects if you have the right tools. I share what has worked for me. When things do not go as planned, consult your cards for advice on the best ways to navigate through any problematic situation. The trick is to keep your connection strong and not allow any fearful or negative thoughts to gain control over you. Do not deny these thoughts and feelings, they have emerged for a reason. Explore them and get to the root cause so they cannot bother you again.

If you get into conflict with someone avoid losing your temper and telling someone exactly what you think and feel about what they said or did. If you are supposed to respond, decide to say something like, "I am sorry you feel that way". When doing this, you are not taking responsibility for their thoughts or feelings but recognising that they think and feel this way.

When someone asks you, "What do you think?" Reply, "I am not sure, let me think about it". If they are insistent, say "This requires careful thought and consideration and I am still processing. It will take me time to give you an answer that will help us resolve this situation". If possible, choose to walk away and decide not to react to the problem. If the other person is looking for an argument, do not give them one.

Be selfish and give yourself some quiet time to be alone with these thoughts and feelings. Take time to consider what was said or done and how it was delivered. Do this while it is still fresh in your mind and take good notes. Do you feel like you have been struck by lightning or were you expecting this to happen? It will be easier to sort out your thoughts and feelings about this event when you understand what is going on. Tell yourself it is OK to feel and think this way, as something upset you. You are a spiritual being having a disappointing human experience. It is also trying to teach you something about yourself through another person's actions. When people show you who they are and how they think and feel, believe them. Their thoughts and feelings are their own and that is how they have chosen to express them.

The way they think and feel is about them and not about you. Remember the spiritual law of reflection, they are saying about you what they think of themselves.

Alternatively, it could reflect the insecurities or worries deep inside of you. Allow theses insecurities to surface and write down all the negative things these thoughts and feelings are telling you. Give yourself time to breathe and process what happened. Turn on some soothing music and get yourself a cup of tea or coffee while writing your notes. It will help you understand what has happened, to figure out what is going on and the best solution.

Once you have completed your notes, take a break and return to them later. Focus on one thing at a time.

Read the first statement or accusation of what was said, take a few deep breaths to center and ground yourself.

Then ask yourself how this makes you feel?
What is going on deep inside you?

Allow these thoughts and feelings to come to the surface.

- Do you think what they said was a misunderstanding?
- Do you feel falsely accused of something?
- Was it how it was delivered that made you feel challenged or insignificant?
- Did you feel powerless?
- Did you feel offended?
- Do you feel sadness or anger as it was not your intention to have this person feel this way about you?

These feelings and more are all valid as they are yours and you need to figure out how you can heal yourself.

It is time to consult your cards. The spread I would use is the five-card spread. It should be able to give you clarity regarding this situation. You can always pull another five cards and lay them in the same position as the others to provide more clarity.

Ask your cards the question, "What do I need to learn from this situation?" Then ask, "How can I heal from this situation?" The question is similar but will offer different insights on how you can figure out what to do.

Here is an excellent question to ask, along with a sample answer. You would ask this one when communications have broken down badly and wonder if it is time to let them go.

For example, "What am I to learn from the breakdown in the relationship?"

What are your first impressions of this spread in answer to this question? My first observation is to run for the hills or stay away from the person in question. You are much better off without this person in your life!

What does this spread tell you? It can be something different, as your intuition might pick up on other things or variations that I did not see. Look at the cards one by one and see how they relate to each other.

The first card the background: Jeopardy. It seems you are taking a risk in trying to fix this breakdown. You may be good for them but they might not be good for you. The question this raises is, how does this person put you at risk?

The second card the present, heart light, tells you to focus on your connection with the divine. Allow it to fill you with divine inspiration and love. Look to love yourself and put your needs before someone else's, as they would not do the same for you. The signs are everywhere that this is not good for you and the more you shine and radiate, the more they will try to put you down.

Meditate daily to keep your intuition strong, so your assessment of people, places situations will be perfect. If you do not, you might not be able to see the wood for the trees.

The third card is the outcome or the result of what will happen when you try to keep this person and the relationship in your life. The card is the Bermuda triangle. It means that if you choose to keep on working on this relationship, expect more of the same, drama and accusations. This person may want you to feel like they have been a victim somehow and perhaps they have been. However, do you want to be their hero?

If your motivation is to help them see life differently and to live a better life sadly, you will fail. Whenever you come up with a solution to help them, they will find a problem with it or tell you they tried it before and it did not work. Unless you like drama and dealing with their problems, one after another without any successful resolution, give this one a miss. This person thrives on being, 'the victim' and doesn't want to change. Try not to buy into their drama and if they ask you an opinion about someone or something your answer should be something like; "I am not sure what to think; what do you think? I was not a witness to what happened, so I am not qualified to give you an opinion. I am sorry you had this experience" and change the conversation.

The fourth card Advice from Spirit: Your Angels and Spirit Guides have your back! It could be why this is coming to light, so you can see this person for who they are. Remember to ask your Angels for help and guidance. Ask them to show you the signs of what you should do. In this case, I feel the message is clear, do you? I think they are saying, stay away from this person. Whenever you need them, say, Angels, please help me now! In this case, ask them to help you understand. Sometimes when someone says they have been a victim of circumstances and someone else was to blame, there is nothing you or I can do to make a difference in this person's life. Sadly, they are happy in their misery and will stay that way until they decide to take responsibility and change it.

The fifth card Advice on how this will affect your everyday life. Caution! Proceed at your own risk. No matter what kind of relationship this is, it is not good for you or in your best interests to keep trying to resolve your differences, as there will always be something else on their list of things for you to do for them. If you continue with this relationship, it will always be on their terms with what works best for them. Walk away and if that is not possible at the moment, plan your escape. Do not blame yourself for being taken in, they told a convincing story and pulled on your heartstrings. It can happen to anyone. You will not be the first person they have taken advantage of and you will probably not be the last.

I bet you did not expect an answer like that. It is all in how you ask the question. You could try asking it differently, for example How can I build an amicable relationship with this person.

You will get a similar answer, perhaps with different cards that offer a slightly different perspective. Consider that some people want to push your buttons and blame you for things beyond your control. There is no sound reason why, this is how they go through life. It has nothing to do with you. If they were not trying to dangle you on a string, they would be dangling someone else. Do not take it personally, it bears no reflection on what you have or have not done.

You were the unsuspecting person they hoodwinked for a while, but not any longer. They do not know how to treat people properly and it is their issue, not yours. Don't beat yourself up about it any longer. There is nothing that you could have done or said that would have changed things.

Practical, intuitive spiritual guidance will work in all areas of your life. Asking the cards questions is not about making you feel good about yourself. It is to help you take positive steps to improve your life. If you want to ask more questions and spend more time on it to find out why this person took you in, you can. When you are ready to let go, let go. You cannot move on while letting this matter rent space in your head. How long do you want to be stuck in limbo? The choice is yours if you were not such a loving person, you would not have been taken advantage of in the first place.

Here are ten deep and meaningful questions that can tell you a lot about yourself. Do not ask them unless you are ready for the answer. These will help you understand how far you have come and where you are on your path. They will help you know what you need to do to work on your spiritual development.

Deep meaningful questions

- Am I in accord with my divine plan?
- What is my major life purpose at this stage in my life?
- Is there negative energy that needs to be removed from my life?
- What past life issues do I need to release?
- What do I need to do to feel worthy of a healthy relationship?
- What do I need to do to attract a loving romantic relationship?
- What will my love life be like when I let go of X
- Why do I attract people who take advantage of me?
- What steps can I take to attract the right kind of people into my life?
- Am I in harmony with the divine by trying to resolve this situation?
- How can I take my power back from this situation?
- Is it wise to trust (name)?
- Is X something I should pursue

Bad things happen to good people

Life is a miracle and wonderful things can happen to us at any point in time. Things happen that knock us down and make us feel defeated and discouraged.

The trick is being grateful for both the good and the bad, so we can learn to live with love, grace and ease. The lessons we learn along the way are a part of our spiritual journey. We can let what happened sour us and keep us down for a while. We can stay stuck in the past, trying to figure it out or let it go and choose to soar.

Embrace your current lesson, it's essential to feel the pain and discomfort and go with it for a while but do not stay there too long. Cry, scream, shout and do what you need to do to embrace this heavy energy. When things go wrong, it's always good to stop what you are doing, clear your head and ask your cards.

"What am I to learn from this situation?"

It could have been a life lesson you could not avoid, but you still get to decide how you grow through it. How does this make you feel what thoughts come to mind?

Do you think this feels like a harsh life lesson?

When you have the insight from the cards, you're becoming aware of options to put your best foot forward in any situation. It is important to remember that you are a divine being having a human experience and try not to take things personally.

Keep your energy high while dealing with what is going on. Avoid slipping down into the lower vibrational energies of this situation when you are furious or feeling injured about something or someone.

You have blocked your connection to your intuitive energy source and will be deaf to any insights it has for you. It is best not to say anything meaningful or hurtful to anyone or make crucial decisions.

Call upon your Angels and Spirit Guides to help you align your energy and take your power back. Do not let others steal your peace and joy.

When we can respond with goodness and mercy, especially when people do not deserve it, it shows that we are centered and grounded and will not be influenced by the whims of others.

Tips that have helped me stay connected when times have been hard

1. Decide every problem is a challenge to be overcome
2. Be brave enough to face your fears and become the master of your destiny
3. Learn when to walk away; some people are just not worth your love or time
4. Laugh at yourself when you repeat the same mistakes and plan to do things differently
5. Success comes with experience and often after lots of failures, so keep trying
6. Do not take life too seriously, we don't get out of it alive
7. Forgive everyone for not being perfect, especially yourself
8. Life changes, so if you do not like what you see now, in no time at all, it will be different
9. When you get knocked down, be kind to yourself, get back up start again
10. This very moment is the perfect time to smile and know that better times are coming
11. Emotional intelligence, do not let someone else's bad mood spoil your day
12. When you set a goal, the next step is to take action and make it happen!

Exercise - The three-card story

I would like you to write a three-card story. Get ready to do a reading and go through your getting ready-to-read process and when you are in the zone, the question your mind should be focused on while shuffling the cards is...

What can you tell me about the frog?

It will become clear later why I am asking you to do this. Look at the cards and write your story based on what intuitively comes to mind. Write as many words about each card as possible. Aiming to write between 150 and 300 words would be best. Stare at the cards and if nothing much comes to you, look up your card meanings for further clarification. Use your intuition as much as possible.

Write what intuitively comes to your mind about this unique frog.

The story starts with: Once upon a time, there was a frog...

I will reveal why this is important at the end of the book.

Once upon a time there was a frog...

What is your life purpose?

Some of us want to know about our life's purpose and how to get on the right path. The answer is that we are always on the right path. We may have paused and taken a break on our journey but we are never off our path.

Sometimes we battle things we thought we should never have had to grow through but it is all part of the plan. There are many major and minor life purposes for all of us, not just one. Ask your cards and they will tell you about your current major life purpose.

I asked the question: "What is my current primary life purpose?"

I decided to use the six-card spread with the wild card. The wild card helps you see something you might not have considered. I shuffled until I felt I had the answer, which seemed to take a while.

I concluded that a big question like this required a lot of shuffling. I am honored by the answer and hope I can help as many people as possible. Here are my thoughts.

Overall impression, I'm supposed to be showing people how to stop sabotaging themselves and clear their path forward. Encourage them to believe in themselves, to get through tough times, to use their intuitive abilities and reclaim their power.

Cards number one and four are the backgrounds as it relates to this question. Help people understand how to make changes in their lives that will be in their best interests. Change can be scary but not as frightening as history that repeats itself. Teach them how to believe in themselves and that life is a miracle. Remind them that they can change their attitude towards what life has brought them anytime they want. These insights will inspire them to make good decisions that will have a ripple effect and create positive changes in their lives.

Cards number two and five, the current situation, the present. Help them overcome problems and pitfalls by teaching them to tune into the divine. It will help keep them out of harm's way and show them how to nourish their intuitive, empathic nature. Show them how to see the signs and hear their angel helpers and messages from spirit guides.

Cards three and six, the outcome or result of this major life purpose. By accepting this mission and doing my best for others, I will help them progress on their journey to reconnect with their divine essence. They will not feel alone and strengthen their connection with their spirit guides and lost loved ones. It will enable them to see the signs and hear messages more clearly, which will help them on their journey through life.

Card Number seven, the wild card. This will help me understand that I will succeed. I am one in a million and it is my destiny to help others connect with the divine. I can help them feel loved and appreciated for becoming their authentic selves, which will help them unleash their divine essence and power.

It is now time to do your own spread with the intention of learning about your current major life purpose.

Different life purposes

When you were a child growing up, your primary life purpose was to be happy. We learn that life is not always fair or just. We are encouraged to tell the truth and be kind, respectful and loving. Life is a school, where each life purpose is a lesson we grow through. If you believe in reincarnation as I do, I understand that we all made a pre-life plan.

We chose this plan to set in motion before we decided to come to the earth and be the person we are today. This plan has many items on its to-do list, which is evident in the one consistent thing about life... it changes. If you do not like what you see in your life today, you are free to change it. Although it may not feel like it at times, we are all masters of our own destiny.

Our primary life purpose changes several times throughout our lifetime. Part of your purpose might be to become a parent, a healer, a caregiver, a teacher, a scientist, an artist or a cleaner. There are no small purposes, they are all significant. You do not know whose life you will touch and inspire.

Consider that some will achieve their life's dream because you inspired them. How about the people you look to for help and advice? Perhaps, these souls chose to motivate and inspire you as part of their purpose!

Think about some of the meaningful things you have done for yourself and others. Consider that these were all part of your life purpose. When we make a spontaneous, random act of kindness, this may cause a ripple effect that could have also been a part of our life purpose.

Take your smile and humility with you wherever you go, as they will help you feel compassion for other people's issues and your current situation. Some people go through life while others grow through life. It is what it is. We can change the world one person at a time, which begins with us.

We were born with the gift of reasoning, which is how we learn along the way. Some people become overwhelmed at times and decide what is going on in their lives has become too much. They decide to take a rain check for the time being or an entire lifetime, the choice is theirs to make. For others, it leads to freedom to think for themselves and not just accept the ideas and beliefs learned growing up.

We acknowledge that there is no supreme religion, culture or way of life. We realize that other people will think and act differently based on what they have learned and believed because no two people are the same.

An excellent simple exercise is to visualize your life as though you were looking at it through the eyes of a small child. When you look at yourself this way, you might feel kinder, more compassionate for the person you are today and in awe at what you have accomplished.

What about when you think you failed? Are these child's eyes critical of you or does this child show concern and compassion? How this child views you will show you how you feel about yourself. Do you need to work on loving yourself a little more or are you contented?

Accepting that you are a spiritual being having a human experience and making mistakes proves that you are alive and living your life to the best of your ability. When we are in the zone, we will have opportunities to rise and prosper and not fall flat on our faces. When you believe you can succeed, you will!

You will be more accepting and less judgemental of the situations you get yourself into when you proceed with the best of intentions. Sometimes things can go wrong in ways that we did not see coming. No one sets out to screw up their lives, yet we do it so magnificently and unwittingly. How often have you said I would have done things differently if I knew what I know now? If we had, would we be where we are at today? Today is the perfect place to capitalize on all those perceived failures, which were lessons we chose to learn.

Success is infectious when others see us doing well, they may adapt and learn from us. I believe our world will be peaceful and happier when more of us overlook other people's imperfections and lend them a hand. Those that want to rise will not want a handout but will appreciate a hand up.

Every one of us has an important role to play in our lives and in the way we touch the lives of others. Your circumstances do not define you. It is your attitude when things go wrong that determines what happens next.

The three-card story answer

The story you wrote about the frog is about you and where you are on your spiritual journey. Reread it several times and substitute the word frog with 'I' you should get some a-ha moments about what is going on in your life and what you can do to change it. If you have any difficulty seeing where you fit into this story, go online to our 6th Sense School on Facebook and post your three-card story and ask for others to tell you what they see. If you enrolled in one of our courses, you could ask for help there too.

I wish you to be all you aspire to be and live your best life filled with love, light happiness. If you have purchased the cards and want to learn more, come and join us in our free Facebook group, where you will have the opportunity to meet and network with more like-minded people.

https://www.facebook.com/groups/6thsenseoracleschool

Please check out my website, **www.6thsenseconnection.com**, for upcoming events, courses, free video lessons and our store!

Until we meet again, wishing you all the very best life can offer!

Love, light and chocolate

About the author

Meet Anne-Marie

Anne-Marie is an author, teacher a celebrated psychic medium with a personality that lights up the room, inspiring fun and giggles. She has been helping people worldwide with her psychic gifts since the 1980s. At an early age, her psychic abilities became apparent. Thankfully she came from a long line of psychic mediums and was able to get the help she needed from her mother and grandmother. She is the founder of 6th Sense Connection, which started as a spiritual store in Cassadaga, Florida. It moved online in 2013, which has enabled her to utilize social media and zoom to teach others how to use their gifts and to do more group and private readings.

She has worked as a psychic medium most of her life and is also a regular business woman. Having a foot in both worlds helps keep her grounded or she might have gone off with the fairies! Her passion is connecting people with Spirit, Angels and higher vibrational energy. She created the 6th Sense Connection Oracle Cards and Workbook to help others expand their intuitive connection to Spirit, work on themselves and do readings.

Anne-Marie believes the future is not cast in stone and we all have free will. The messages from Spirit and the oracle cards come with humor, kindness, honesty and compassion. She believes the one consistent thing about life is that it changes. If you do not like your current circumstances, it is never too late to laugh at life and do something positive. All you need is a little know-how and a nudge in the right direction to become the master of your destiny. Anne-Marie decided long ago that no matter what comes her way, she will embrace it emotionally by saying WTF and then transform that energy with love and gratitude. She lives close to family and friends in the UK with her husband. Anne-Marie's hobbies include exploring mystical arts, crystals, writing, gardening, baking and dancing!

Learn more & keep in touch at **www.6thsenseconnection.com**

www.ingramcontent.com/pod-product-compliance
Lightning Source LLC
Chambersburg PA
CBHW051552010526
44118CB00022B/2669